DO-IT-YOURSELF GUIDES

Step-By-Step
Exterior Repairs

Quality tools to build your world.

ACKNOWLEDGEMENTS

Created by Creative Publishing international
in conjunction with WSP Marketing International Ltd.,
47 Valleybrook Drive, Don Mills, Ontario M3B 2S6,
Canada.

**Creative Publishing international
Book Development Staff**

Vikki Anderson
Shawn Binkowski
Steve Boman
Janice Cauley
Marcia Chambers
Maren Christensen
Paul Currie
Doug Deutscher
Melissa Erickson
Jacque Fletcher
John Fletcher
Brad Kissell
Janet Lawrence
Bill Nelson
Chuck Nields
Jon Simpson
Greg Wallace
Gina Wornson

Printed on Canadian paper by World Color
Book Services, USA.

ISBN 0-86573-761-4

This book provides useful instructions but
we cannot anticipate all of your working
conditions or the characteristics of your
materials and tools. For safety, you should
use caution, care and good judgement
when following the procedures described in
this book. Consider your own skill level and
the instructions and safety precautions
associated with the various tools and
materials shown.

Creative Publishing international, WSP
Marketing International Ltd., Canadian Tire
Corporation, Ltd., or the Canadian Tire
Associate Dealers do not assume any
responsibility for damage to property
or injury to persons as a result of the use
of the information contained in this book.

Before commencing any project, consult
your local Building Department for information on building permits, codes and other
laws, as they may apply to your project.

INTRODUCTION

The exterior of your home takes a constant beating from the weather. There are always repairs needed to the roof, eavestroughs, siding or masonry structures due to the harsh effects of the sun, wind, rain and freezing temperatures. These repairs can be costly, especially if you must hire professionals to do the work. *Step-By-Step Exterior Repairs* will help you do this work yourself and will save you both time and money. This book will guide you through the most common repairs needed on the outside of your home. You'll see which Mastercraft tools you need and the proper techniques for using them, as well as information about the best materials to choose for your repair projects.

Step-By-Step Exterior Repairs is divided into sections covering major areas of exterior home repair. Each section contains the kind of information you need to know before beginning repair projects, including how to work safely and any work area preparations you may need to make. Then, individual projects are demonstrated with detailed, step-by-step instructions and full-colour photographs. You'll also see the specific tools and materials each project requires. Throughout each section you will find tips about tools, materials and project techniques that will make your work as simple and efficient as possible.

Now you can keep your home in good repair – and save time and money, too. Welcome to the world of Mastercraft Do-It-Yourself Guides!

TABLE OF CONTENTS

Tools, Checklist & Safety 6

Using Caulk & Wood Fillers . . 10

Siding & Trim Repairs. 12

Painting Exterior Surfaces . . . 18

Brick & Block Care & Repair . . 28

Concrete Care & Repair 37

Repairing Eavestroughs 48

Roof Repairs 52

Deck Repair 58

Index. 62

TOOLS, CHECKLIST & SAFETY

To successfully make the repair projects seen in this book you need the proper tools, and they are shown here. Quality tools, like Mastercraft, will serve your needs well. Keep hand tools protected and organized by storing them in a toolbox. This also will allow you to easily carry them to the project site. Shelves or cabinets are good locations for power tools and other specialty tools and supplies.

Basic hand tools: *caulk gun (A), putty knife (B), pry bar/nail puller (C), work gloves (D), ear protection (E), carpenter's square (F), level (G), work light (H), chisels (I), sponge (J), eye protection (K), pencil (L), felt-tipped pen (M), mallet (N), hammer (O), awl (P), file (Q), nail set (R), dust mask (S), chalk line (T), hex key wrenches (U), utility knife (V), sandpaper (W), needlenose pliers (X), Robo-Grip® pliers (Y), groove joint pliers (Z), screwdrivers (AA), clamps – bar & C (BB), hacksaw (CC), tape measure (DD), scissors (EE), handsaw (FF), stud finder (GG), straightedge (HH).*

Power tools: *circular saw (A), drill, cordless or corded (B), jigsaw (C), palm sander (D), drill bits, including screwdriver bits (E), wire wheel (F), heat gun (G).*

Other tools: *hand maul (A), wood float (B), trowel (C), hydraulic jack (D), masonry grinding wheel (E), roofing blade (F), aviator snips (G), ratchet wrench and socket (H), pop rivet (I).*

| GOOD | FAIR | POOR | # Exterior House Maintenance Checklist |

ROOF, EAVESTROUGHS, SOFFITS & FASCIA

Shingles:	❏ buckling ❏ damage ❏ exposed nails	❏ cupping ❏ missing shingles	❏ wear ❏ leaks
Flashing:	❏ deterioration	❏ loose or detached	❏ bad seals
Chimney:	❏ loose masonry	❏ soot build-up	❏ pests
Eavestroughs:	❏ leaks or holes ❏ clogs	❏ sags	❏ rust or deterioration
Soffits & fascia:	❏ rot	❏ cracks or damage	❏ pests

SIDING & TRIM

Siding:	❏ rot/damage ❏ buckling	❏ missing siding	❏ paint failure
Trim:	❏ rot/damage	❏ cracks/splits	❏ paint failure

DOORS & WINDOWS

Weatherstripping:	❏ damaged	❏ missing	
Hardware:	❏ rust/corrosion ❏ misaligned	❏ paint failure	❏ sticking
Glass & screening:	❏ broken/torn	❏ glazing/retaining strips deteriorated	
Frames, wood:	❏ rot/damage	❏ paint failure	

FOUNDATION

Leaks:	❏ water in basement	❏ condensation on interior walls	
General condition:	❏ small cracks	❏ large cracks	❏ deterioration

DECKS, PORCHES & PATIOS

Wood surfaces:	❏ rot/damage	❏ paint failure	❏ loose boards
Masonry surfaces:	❏ cracks	❏ stains	❏ concrete failure
Railings, trim, accessories:	❏ rust/paint failure	❏ rot/damage	

DRIVEWAY & SIDEWALKS

Driveway:	❏ cracks	❏ stains	❏ damage
Sidewalks:	❏ cracks	❏ stains	❏ damage

SECURITY

Lighting:	❏ burned-out bulbs	❏ unlit entries	
Locks:	❏ operate smoothly	❏ window locks	❏ strike plate aligned
General:	❏ entries unobscured	❏ security system functional	

Working Safely

Thorough preparation and thoughtful anticipation of conditions you may encounter will ensure your personal safety and the ultimate success of a project.

Work with a helper whenever you can or let someone know you are working outside. Never work at heights or with power tools if you have consumed alcohol or medication. Do not work in stormy or windy weather. If you are working at heights, consider using a safety harness that attaches to the roof. Plan for easy disposal of waste materials such as old nails, jagged metal from flashing and piles of old shingles. Create a centrally located storage surface for tools to keep them out of your way and protect them from moisture.

When working outside and using electricity, connect to a GFCI-protected receptacle, or use a GFCI extension cord that shuts off power if a short circuit occurs (often from water contact). Use cordless tools when possible.

Tips for Ladder Safety

❏ Watch for wires, branches and overhangs when moving ladders.

❏ Drill a hole and secure a clip bolt or another type of fastener to the top of your ladder for tying off power cords or air hoses. The weight of a power cord or hose is enough to pull most power tools off the roof.

❏ Use extreme caution when working near electrical service cables. Use only wood or fibreglass ladders.

❏ Use an extension ladder for making quick repairs to fascia, eavestroughs and soffits, and to gain roof access. For larger projects like painting walls, use scaffolding.

❏ Provide level, stable footing for ladders and scaffolding. Install sturdy blocking under the legs of ladders. If ground is soft, wet or slippery, drive a stake behind ladder feet.

❏ Attach ladder boots and an adjustable ladder stabilizer to your ladder to minimize slipping. Rest stabilizer feet against broad, flat stable surfaces (photo above).

❏ Never carry heavy items up an extension ladder. Use a hoist to raise items to the roof.

❏ Position extension ladders so the flat tops of the D-shaped rungs are facing up, parallel to the ground.

❏ Extend the ladder three feet above the roof edge for greater stability and gripping.

USING CAULK & WOOD FILLERS

Caulk has many uses around the home. By filling gaps, cracks and holes of every variety, caulk blocks air movement to help conserve energy. It also prevents damage by sealing moisture out of wall cavities and other areas. For general exterior purposes, use siliconized acrylic or latex caulk. These products are flexible, long-lasting, paintable, water-resistant and relatively inexpensive. Other types of caulk include peel-and-stick caulk, roofing mastic, butyl-base caulk, butyl driveway patch and latex masonry patch.

RECOMMENDED HAND TOOLS

- wood chisel
- putty knife
- wood file
- caulk gun
- paintbrush

NEEDED MATERIALS

- wood forms
- caulk
- exterior-rated wood filler
- sandpaper
- paint or stain

Wood Fillers

Use two-part epoxy wood fillers or other exterior-rated fillers to repair wood siding and trim. Do not use standard wood putty; it is not rated for exterior use.

Remember that the thickness of the layer applied can vary between products, so follow the directions on the label.

How to Apply Wood Filler

1 Remove damaged or rotted wood using a wood chisel or utility knife.

2 Brush away debris, then wash the area.

3 For larger repair areas, attach wood forms to help shape the filler.

4 Prepare the filler for application (see manufacturer's directions), then apply it with a putty knife.

5 Once the filler has dried, sand with 150-grit sandpaper to shape contours and create a smooth surface. Use a wood file for more extensive shaping.

6 Paint or stain to match surrounding wood.

Applying Caulk

Cut out old caulk with a utility knife and clean the surface. Cut the tip of the caulk tube at a 45° angle. Puncture the tube seal before loading the tube into your caulk gun.

Squeeze the trigger to bring caulk to the tube's tip. Draw a continuous bead, then release the plunger and pull gun away from worksurface. Use caulking backer rope for cracks wider than 1/4".

Masonry Cracks & Mortar Replacement

As with all other caulking applications, the first step is to remove loose material when repairing masonry. Use a chisel and wire brush, then clean surfaces with a brush or hand vacuum. Use a caulk gun to apply masonry patch to a crack. Latex fillers are especially easy to apply and clean up. Although convenient, repair caulk should be viewed only as a short-term solution to improve appearance and help prevent further damage from water penetration. After filling the crack, smooth out the caulk with a putty knife, trowel or wooden dowel.

When replacing mortar, chip out loose material with a masonry chisel and ball peen hammer. Clean cracks with a wire brush or hand vacuum. Mix fresh mortar and apply to cracks with a pointed trowel. Smooth out mortar and then clean the brick face with a brush and a 5% muriatic acid solution.

Repairing Stucco

Pre-mixed stucco repair compound can be used for patching small holes or crumbled areas of stucco. Use concrete or stucco repair caulk for filling small cracks (photo below). Over-fill a crack with caulk and then feather it until flush with the stucco. When patching holes, clean out area, remove any rust from exposed metal lath and then use a metal primer to treat the lath. Trowel pre-mixed stucco into area and smooth out. Use a whisk broom to create a matching texture on the stucco patch and use masonry paint to blend in the repair.

Sealing Holes & Cracks in Walls

- ❑ **Caulk windows and doors** with a good-quality latex or silicone caulk to prevent rotting of wood and to reduce heat loss.
- ❑ **Caulk around wires and pipes** entering the house. Remove old, cracked caulk before applying new, coloured caulk that matches siding.
- ❑ **Caulk the mud sill,** which is the horizontal wooden plate where the house rests on the foundation.
- ❑ **Stuff fibreglass insulation** into large holes and cracks to provide a base for the caulk. Fibreglass also insulates.
- ❑ **Caulk under shingles** with a good-quality roof mastic, and coat nail heads to prevent leaks after replacing roof shingles.
- ❑ **Caulk roof flashings** around chimneys, vents and skylights with roof mastic.

TIP:
Muriatic acid is highly corrosive and can easily burn skin. Be sure to wear protective clothing like Mastercraft safety goggles and acid-resistant work gloves when working with it.

SIDING & TRIM REPAIRS

TIP:

Many homes built in the 1940s and the 1950s were covered with milled asbestos shingles. Asbestos shingles have the same general appearance as fibreglass, usually with a rough, heavily ridged surface. Because asbestos is classified as a hazardous material, its handling and disposal are regulated. Contact your local waste management department before handling asbestos shingles.

No matter how much exterior house coverings have improved over the years, the wear and tear from the environment and our own daily living patterns ensure that all types of siding and trim will continue to need some maintenance or repair occasionally.

Repairing Siding & Trim

Traditional wood lap siding can be repaired quite easily. Epoxy-based wood fillers and long-lasting caulk products make the task easy. And replacing missing or damaged wood shingles or shakes is among the simplest exterior home repairs.

Like brick veneer and stucco, masonry siding repairs no longer need to be relegated to a skilled, professional mason. Masonry siding can be repaired with a few easy-to-apply products.

The most significant change in siding maintenance and repair has come with "low maintenance" or "no maintenance" manufactured siding products. Aluminum, vinyl and steel siding products have become commonplace in the past few decades. When they first hit the market, repair of these products was done exclusively by licensed contractors; now, most building centres carry a range of replacement parts and repair products.

Siding damage, *like the water damage from the leaky hose bib shown above, often requires replacement of the affected siding pieces. First, find and repair the source of the damage.*

TIP:

If the damage to your siding (whatever the type) is so extensive that it requires full replacement, consider hiring a contractor. Few home improvement projects are more time-consuming than applying new siding – especially if you are installing products that you have never worked with before. There is a lot of competition among siding contractors, and you can usually come up with a range of bids. But as with any bid, do not look only at the cost. Whenever hiring a contractor, check references and licenses, and obtain written estimates.

Evaluating Siding & Trim

The first step in inspecting and evaluating siding and trim is to identify the material types. Common siding types include:

Wood lap siding. This is usually made of cedar, pine or hardwood particleboard. Bevelled boards are the most common. Wood lap is very easy to repair.

Vinyl siding. This type is virtually maintenance free. Minor repairs can be made with caulk or patches. Contact a siding contractor before making major repairs.

Metal siding. Minor patching and caulking can take care of many common problems affecting metal siding. Contact a contractor for major repairs.

Shakes & shingles. Shakes and shingles usually are cut from cedar or pine. Basic repairs are easy on wood shakes and shingles.

Brick. Small problems in brick veneer can be repaired with quick-fix concrete repair products. For major repairs, contact an expert.

Stucco. Minor repairs can be made with concrete or stucco repair products. For wide cracks and major damage, call an expert.

Inspecting Trim

When evaluating trim pieces, keep in mind that some can be removed to make repairs easier.

Window and door trim. Carefully inspect for rot on horizontal surfaces and at joints in particular. In this case, try to make repairs without removing the trim.

Decorative trim. Detailed, decorative trim pieces like gingerbread trim, for example, can be removed if you suspect damage. You will find repairs much easier in the workshop.

Broad trim pieces. Broad trim such as end caps can be repaired using the same techniques you would use with siding.

Common Siding Problems

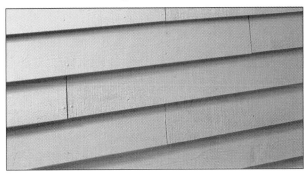 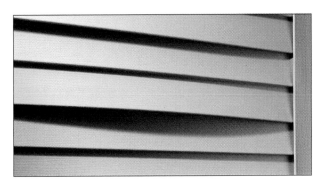

*Separated joints (photo above left) occur in any type of lap siding but are most common in wood. Gaps between 1/8" and 1/4" thick can be filled with caulk. Gaps 3/8" or wider could mean that your house has a serious moisture or shifting problem. **Buckling** (photo above right) occurs most frequently in manufactured siding, when expansion gaps are too small at the points where the siding fits into trim and channels. If possible, move the channel slightly; if not, remove the siding, trim the length slightly and then reinstall. In those cases where you have **minor surface damage** on metal siding, it's often best to leave it alone unless the damage has penetrated the surface. With metal products, cosmetic surface repairs often look worse than the damage. Immediately replace **missing siding.** While you are at it, check surrounding siding to make sure it is secure.*

MASTERCRAFT

CIRCULAR SAW

RECOMMENDED HAND TOOLS

MASTERCRAFT

BASIC HAND TOOLS

- chisel
- trowel
- hacksaw
- keyhole saw
- pry bar
- nail set
- stud finder
- paintbrush

NEEDED MATERIALS

- epoxy wood filler
- epoxy glue
- nails and deck screws
- siliconized acrylic caulk
- plastic roof cement
- building paper
- lumber crayon
- sheathing
- wood preservative
- primer
- paint or stain

Stagger vertical seams *to make your siding repairs less visible. Where possible, drive fasteners into framing members. Exterior sheathing or underlayment is often made from composite materials that may not hold fasteners well.*

Repairing Siding

Unless your home has sustained extremely severe damage, you will have little trouble doing routine repairs to common types of siding. A well-executed siding repair not only wards off more serious structural problems but adds to the visual appeal of your home – especially if the repair materials are a good blend with the surrounding siding.

For small to medium holes, cracks, rotted areas and indentations in siding, use an appropriate filler. For major siding damage, you may have to remove and replace affected siding pieces. Be sure to number siding pieces as you remove them. Templates for replacement pieces can be made from the boards you remove.

If you cannot find matching siding at building centres, check with salvage yards or siding contractors. When repairing aluminum or vinyl siding, contact the manufacturer or the contrac-

tor who installed the siding to help you locate matching materials and parts. If you cannot find an exact match, remove original siding from a less-visible area of your house – like the back of the garage – and use it as the patch. In the less-visible area, use the near-match siding to patch the gap.

Before attaching new siding, be sure to patch building paper that also may have been damaged. When applying a patch, loosen the building paper above the damaged area and slip the top of the patch underneath. Attach the patch with staples. Use roof cement to patch small holes or tears.

When repairing lap siding, insert spacers between siding and sheathing above the work area. This creates better access and simplifies repairs. When removing metal siding, do not bend it too far or it will buckle.

Repairing & Replacing Wood Siding

Of the many siding types available, wood-based products are easiest to repair. Just remember to use only exterior-rated wood and wood repair products.

Repair cracks and splits in wood siding with epoxy wood glue. Apply the glue to both sides of the crack, then press the board back together. For best results, position a board under the bottom edge of the damaged board and press it upward to create even pressure until the glue sets. (If working near the ground, wedge a 2x4 under the board for this purpose.) Next, drive galvanized deck screws into each side of the crack to reinforce the repair. Clean off any excess glue and touch up the repair with paint. If damage is too great to repair, use the following steps to replace siding.

How To Replace Wood Siding

1 Use an electronic stud finder to locate and mark framing members around repair area. Mark cut-out lines over the centers of framing members on each side of repair area. Stagger lines so vertical joints do not align.

2 Insert spacers beneath the board above the repair area. Use a keyhole saw to make entry cuts at the tops of the cutting lines; then saw through the boards with the saw in an upright position. Remove the boards. Remove any nails.

3 Measure and cut all replacement boards to fit, leaving an expansion gap of 1/8" at each end. Apply preservative/sealer or primer to board ends and back sides before installation.

4 Nail the new boards in place with ring-shank siding nails, starting with the lowest board. Drive nails into framing members using the original nailing pattern (normally at 12" intervals through the bottom of the exposed board and the top of the board below).

How To Replace Shakes & Shingles

1 Split damaged shakes or shingles with a hammer and chisel, and remove. Insert wood spacers under the shakes or shingles above the repair area, then slip a hacksaw blade under the top board to cut off any nail heads remaining from the old shake or shingle.

2 Cut replacement shakes or shingles to fit, leaving a 1/8"- to 1/4"-wide expansion gap at each side. Coat all sides and edges with wood preservative. Slip the patch pieces under the siding above the repair area (start on lower courses if patching a large area). Attach with ring-shank siding nails, driven near the top of the exposed area on the patch. Cover all nail heads with caulk, wiping off any excess. Remove spacers.

Create an expansion gap *at seams between wood siding panels or lap siding. Use a nail as a guide to set gap widths. (For most siding types, 1/8" is an adequate expansion gap.) Fill the gaps with exterior caulk.*

5 Fill expansion joints with caulk (use paintable caulk for painted wood, and tinted caulk for stained wood), then prime and paint or stain the replacement siding boards to match the surrounding boards.

TIP:

A zip tool is used to separate and connect vinyl and metal siding pieces. If you cannot find one elsewhere, you should be able to purchase one where these types of siding are sold.

Repairing Vinyl & Metal Siding

Vinyl and metal exterior products are relatively inexpensive and can last for decades. Minor repairs can be done by do-it-yourselfers. Call a professional for major work.

How To Patch Vinyl Siding

1 Unlock interlocking joints with the siding above the repair area, using a zip tool (photo below). Start unlocking at the seam nearest the damaged area. Install spacers below the piece above, then pry out fasteners in the top piece of damaged siding, using a pry bar.

2 Cut out damaged area with a straightedge and utility knife; then cut from similar material a replacement piece 4" longer than the open area. Trim off 2" of the nailing strip from replacement piece ends in the overlap area. Slide into position.

3 Attach replacement siding. Drive nails by rapping on pry bar neck with a hammer.

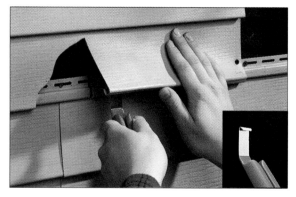

Vinyl and metal siding pieces *have a locking J-channel that fits over the bottom of the nailing strip on the piece below. Use a zip tool (photo inset) to separate siding panels. Insert zip tool at the overlapping seam nearest repair area. Slide the zip tool over the J-channel, pulling outward slightly to unlock joint from siding below (photo above).*

How To Patch Metal Siding

1 Use aviator snips and a hacksaw to remove damaged areas. Leave some exposed surface at the top of uppermost piece removed to serve as bonding surface for the top patch.

2 Cut patches 4" wider than the repair area, using like material. Cut off nailing strip from top of top patch piece. Smooth edges with metal sandpaper.

3 Drive ring-shank nails through the nailing strip to secure lower patches, starting with the lowest piece. For the top piece, apply roofing cement and press the patch in place, slipping the J-shaped locking channel over the nailing strip below. Caulk seams.

How To Replace Aluminium Caps

1 Remove damaged end caps. If caps cannot be removed easily, pry bottom loose, then cut along the top with a hacksaw.

2 Attach replacement end caps, starting at the bottom. Drive ring-shank siding nails through nailing tabs and into framing members.

3 Trim nailing tabs off top replacement cap, then apply roofing cement to the back. Snap cap over J-shaped locking channels of the siding courses. Press top cap securely in place.

Repairing Trim

While some trim like gingerbread or ornate cornice mouldings serves a decorative purpose, other trim serves a more practical need. Brick moulding and corner boards should be patched with stock material similar to the original. If you cannot find matching replacement parts for trim, check salvage shops or contact a custom millworker.

Repairing Corner Boards

Reattach loose trim with new ring-shank siding nails driven near old nail locations (photo above). Fill old nail holes with paintable caulk, and touch up caulk and new nail heads with paint to match. In the case of delicate ornamental trim moulding, however, you will find it easier to repair while it is still attached.

How to Replace Brick Moulding

1 Pry off old brick moulding around windows and doors using a flat pry bar. Remove any old drip edge. Inspect and repair building paper as necessary.

2 Hold a replacement piece of brick moulding, slightly longer than the original piece, across the opening. Mark cutting lines to fit the opening (photo below). Cut the replacement moulding at cutting lines, matching any mitre cuts.

3 Cut a 3" wide piece of flashing to fit between the jambs; bend it in half lengthwise to form a new drip edge. (Pre-formed drip edge is available.) Slip it between siding and building paper, above the door or window. Do not nail the drip edge in place.

4 Test-fit the replacement piece of brick moulding. Apply and let set exterior-grade panel adhesive to the back side.

5 Nail brick moulding to door header with 10d galvanized casing nails. Lock-nail mitre joints and set nail heads. Seal joints and cover nail holes with caulk. Prime and paint when caulk dries.

PAINTING EXTERIOR SURFACES

Blistering *can result from poor preparation or hasty application of primer or paint.*

Peeling *is often a result of ongoing moisture problems due to leaks or failed vapour barrier.*

Alligatoring *is due to excess layers, poor surface preparation or too little primer drying time.*

Stained walls and fascia *are often caused by eavestroughs that leak or overflow when clogged.*

When prepared and applied correctly, an exterior paint job can last a decade or more. But before you even lift a paintbrush, the most critical step awaits you: proper and thorough preparation of the surface for priming and the finish coat.

It is best to tackle just one side of your house at a time. This helps limit the time your siding is exposed after scraping and sanding – preparations which can cause plugged wood pores and, ultimately, a poor bond with the paint. Prime and paint as soon as you finish preparation.

By touching up minor chipping or localized flaking as they occur, you can prevent water build-up under the surface and mildew formation that leads to staining and paint failure. Pressure washing your siding should be a key annual maintenance project, but do not damage the surface by getting too close.

Evaluating Painted Surfaces

Blistering describes paint that bubbles as trapped moisture forces its way through the surface. Scrape and touch up localized blistering. For widespread damage, remove paint down to bare wood, then apply new primer and paint.

Peeling occurs when paint disengages entirely from the surface, falling away in flakes. To correct such problems, scrape and sand localized damage, then touch up with primer and paint. Widespread damage calls for removing paint down to bare wood and then refinishing.

Alligatoring is widespread flaking and cracking of surfaces, typically seen on old paint and surfaces with many layers of paint. Remove paint down to bare wood and refinish.

Check sheltered areas first. *Initial signs of paint failure in areas that receive little or no direct sunlight are a warning sign that neighbouring areas may be in danger of similar paint failure.*

Stained walls and fascias occur when water backs up from clogged eavestroughs, or if they leak. Eavestroughs overflow if they are plugged with leaves and debris. To correct the problem, clear or fix downspouts and eavestroughs.

Detecting the Source of Moisture Beneath a Painted Surface

Localized blistering and peeling indicate that moisture, usually from a leaky roof or eavestrough system, is trapped under the paint. Check roofing and eavestrough materials to find the source of the leak. You might also look for leaking pipes inside the wall. Correct the moisture problem before you repaint.

Clearly defined blistering and peeling occurs on exterior surfaces when a humid room, like a bathroom, has an insufficient vapour barrier between the interior and exterior walls. If there is a clear line where an interior wall ends, you probably will need to remove the wall coverings and replace the vapour barrier. In some cases, you may be able to solve the problem by increasing ventilation or adding a dehumidifier.

Safe Handling of Lead Paint

Lead-based paint is a hazard in homes built before 1960. If your house is of this vintage, before scraping and sanding you should test the paint for lead using a lead-testing kit.

Call your local building inspector or waste management department for information on handling and disposing of lead paint.

Identifying Common Surface Problems

Mildew forms in cracks and in humid areas with little direct sunlight. Wash with 1:1 solution of household chlorine bleach and water, or with TSP (trisodium phosphate), to kill the mildew.

Bleeding occurs when nails in siding "pop" and turn rusty. Remove the nails, sand out the rust and drive in new ring-shank siding nails. Apply metal primer, then paint to match.

Rust occurs when moisture penetrates paint on iron or steel. Remove rust and loose paint with a portable drill wire brush, then prime and repaint.

Efflorescence occurs in masonry when minerals leech through the surface, forming a crystalline or powdery layer. Use muriatic acid to remove before painting.

> **TIP:**
> The relatively small added investment it takes to use quality primer and house paint will make your hard work last for years longer than if you use cheaper products. You will also find that high-quality preparation and application tools are a good investment because they produce better results with less work.
>
> Traditionally, almost all house paint has been oil-based. But new latex-based products now rival oil-based products in durability and appearance, without the hazards, odours, clean-up and disposal problems of oil-based paints.
>
> Useful painting materials include tarps, wire scrapers, TSP, masking tape, sandpaper, caulk, primers (tinted to match the paint colour) and, of course, the paint you select.

ESTIMATING YOUR PAINT NEEDS PER COAT

Add: square footage of walls (length x height), square footage of soffit panels and 15% allowance for waste.
Subtract: square footage of doors and windows.

To determine the number of litres or gallons needed, divide total square footage by the coverage rate (on paint-can label).

Preparing for Painting

The more preparation work you do prior to painting, the smoother and longer-lasting the finished surface will be. You will be happy to find, however, that there is a point of diminishing returns when it comes to preparation. Experience will help you decide how much sanding and scraping is enough to not only meet your aesthetic expectations but produce a lasting, durable finish.

In all cases you will want to remove and spot-sand all paint that has completely lost its bond with the surface.

Pressure washing is an important element in surface maintenance and paint preparation. All painted surfaces should receive this thorough cleaning. A rotating scrub brush also can be attached to clean hard-to-reach areas like cornices and soffits. You may want to lay out plastic tarps to collect the residue from this washing.

For the smoothest finish, *sand all the way to bare wood with a Master-craft finishing sander (A). For a less time-consuming (but rougher) finish, scrape, then spot-sand the rough edges (B). Pressure washing alone removes some flaky paint, but it will not create a satisfactory finish (C).*

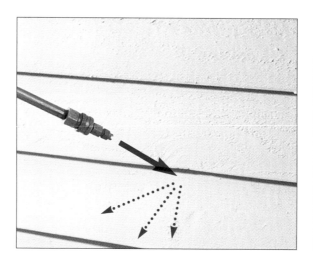

TIP:

When pressure washing siding, direct the water stream at a downward angle (photo left). Avoid getting too close to the surface with the sprayer head to prevent damage to the siding or trim due to the force of the stream of water. When pressure washing high on a wall, use an extension attachment.

How To Prepare Surfaces for Paint

1 Pressure washing cleans the surface and dislodges loose paint. Allow the house to dry before continuing the preparation work.

2 Use a paint scraper to get off loose paint that was not removed during the pressure washing. Be careful not to damage the surface with overly aggressive scraping. Use a flat file to sharpen the edge occasionally.

3 Remove loose paint in hard-to-reach areas with a detail scraper.

4 Use a palm sander with 80-grit sandpaper to smooth out rough paint.

5 Use sanding blocks and 80- to 120-grit sandpaper to remove paint and smooth ridges. Purchase or make your own blocks from dowels, wood scraps, garden hose or other household materials.

6 Check surfaces closely for cracks, rot or other damage. Mark damaged areas with coloured pushpins or tape so you can find them when making the repairs.

7 Use caulk, wood fillers or other appropriate materials to repair cracks, holes and other damage (see pages 10 – 11).

8 Use a finishing sander with 120-grit sandpaper to sand down ridges and hard edges left from the scraping process, creating a smooth surface.

9 Use a coarse abrasive pad or 150-grit sandpaper to scuff-sand glossy surfaces on doors, window casings and surfaces painted with enamel. This creates better bonding surfaces.

10 Use paintable, siliconized caulk for filling cracks in siding and gaps around windows and doors.

Methods for Paint Removal

You may want to completely strip paint off a surface. This may be the case when the accumulation over the years of many layers of paint has created a rough and unwork-able surface, or if you are working with delicate trim pieces. Here are some options:

Heat Gun. This is used to loosen thick layers of paint. Aim the gun at the surface and move it constantly in order to avoid burning the materials. Follow with a scraper once the material releases. Read manufacturer's directions and precautions.

Chemical Stripper. Use stripper to remove paint from delicate trim pieces, following directions on the container. Use heavy-duty rubber gloves and work in well-ventilated areas.

Portable Drill with Sanding Disk. This tool removes large areas of paint on wood lap siding. Select a disk with the same diameter as the width of the reveal area on your siding.

Removing Clear Finishes

Pressure wash stained or unpainted surfaces that have been treated with a wood preservative or protectant before recoating with fresh sealant. Clear topcoats and sealants can flake and peel like paint.

Use a stiff-bristled brush to dislodge any flakes of loosened surface coating not removed by pressure washing. Do not use a wire brush on wood because it could mar the surface.

Hard-to-reach areas *can be made less difficult with a detail scraper. Some have interchangeable heads that match your trim profiles.*

Removing Paint from Metal & Masonry

Taking paint off of metal and masonry calls for a whole different set of techniques than those used for wood surfaces. With metal, use a wire brush to remove loose paint and rust from metal hardware like railings and ornate trim. Cover the surface with metal primer immediately after brushing to prevent new rust from forming.

Scuff-sand metal siding and trim with medium-coarse steel wool or a coarse abrasive pad. Wash the surface before priming and painting.

Masonry surfaces may also require the use of wire brushes and drill attachments. Make sure to clean and power wash the surface thoroughly before painting.

Remove rust from metal hardware *with diluted muriatic acid solution. Be sure to use caution when working with muriatic acid: wear safety equipment, work in a ventilated area and follow the manufacturer's directions and precautions.*

Use a Mastercraft drill with a wire-wheel attachment *to remove loose mortar, mineral deposits or paint from mortar lines in masonry surfaces. Clean broad, flat surfaces with a wire brush. Correct any minor damage with masonry repair products.*

TIP:
All surface preparation work – whether sanding, scraping, steel brushing or removing rust with acid – poses a hazard to your eyes. Mastercraft has four different styles of safety glasses, in addition to adjustable full-face protectors used for welding and other projects. Styles that cover eyes from all angles will go the farthest in protecting your eyes.

Painting Tips & Techniques

Once you have gone the distance in providing a solid base for a finish coat, a little extra planning and effort is all it will take to ensure quality results during actual priming and painting. Here are some basic tips:

❏ If you use a quality primer that is tinted to closely match the colour of your house paint, you can often achieve good coverage with only one finish coat.

❏ Remember that cold weather, damp conditions or rain that falls within an hour or two of application will likely ruin your paint job. Check the paint manufacturer's recommended temperature and drying times printed on the can.

❏ Try to avoid working in high winds. Not only is this unsafe, but dust and dirt could blow onto the freshly painted surface.

❏ Apply primer and paint in the shade or indirect sunlight. Direct sunlight dries primers and paints too rapidly, causing moisture to become trapped below the dried surface. This can result in blistering, peeling and other types of paint failure. Lap and brush marks are also more likely to show up if paint is applied in direct sunlight.

In all cases, use the best primer or paint you can afford. For optimum results, use a metal primer with rust inhibitor for metal surfaces, and use masonry primer with an anti-chalking additive for masonry surfaces. Always read manufacturer's recommendations for use.

Paint downward from the top of your house. *After the primer or paint dries, return to each section and touch up any unpainted areas that were covered by the pads of the ladder or ladder stabilizer.*

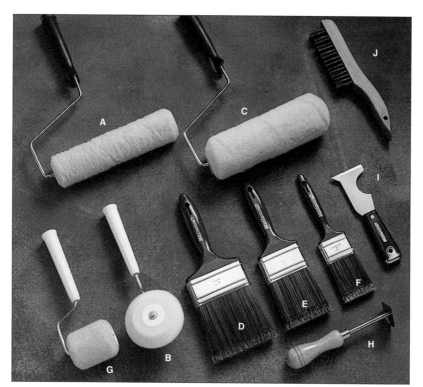

Tools for applying primer and paint *include: a roller and sleeve with a ³/₈" nap for semi-smooth surfaces (A); a corner roller for corners and trim (B); a roller with a ⁵/₈" nap for rough surfaces (C); a 4" paintbrush for lap siding (D); a 3" brush for siding and trim (E); a 2" angle sash brush for trim and window frames (F); and a 3"-wide roller for trim (G); detail scraper (H); combination paint scraper (I); wire brush (J).*

Options for Applying Primer & Paint

There are basically three types of applicators – each specially designed for one of the wide variety of surfaces and shapes on most homes.

Paintbrushes. When maximum control is needed, use a brush. Have clean 2½", 3" and 4" brushes on hand, as well as a tapered sash brush.

Paint Rollers. To paint smooth surfaces quickly, use a roller. Use one that has an 8" or 9" roller sleeve for broad surfaces, and a 3"-wide roller for flat-surfaced trim.

Power Sprayer. These can not be beat when you are working with hard-to-paint surfaces like porch railings, ornate trim and various forms of metal hardware. Keep in mind that professional-quality airless sprayers can be rented for large spray-painting projects.

How To Paint Flat Surfaces

1 Load your brush with a full load of paint. Starting at one end, make a long, smooth stroke until the paint begins to "feather" out. As you finish the stroke, gradually lift the brush from the surface so you do not leave a definite ending point. If the paint appears uneven or contains heavy brush marks, smooth it out. Be careful to avoid overbrushing.

2 Reload your brush and make another stroke from the other direction, painting over the feathered end of the first stroke to create a smooth, even surface.

TIP:
Mastercraft One Coat brushes come in both synthetic and natural bristles. Synthetic-bristle brushes work well for both latex and oil-based paints, but natural-bristle brushes only can be used with oil-based paints. The One Coat Supreme synthetic brush spreads paint faster than most brushes.

Working with Brushes

Pattern the amount of paint you use on your brush to the size and detail of the surface you are painting. Use a full load for broad areas, a moderate load for smaller areas and feathering strokes, and a light load when painting or working around trim. Hold the paintbrush at a 45° angle when painting broad, flat areas. Apply just enough downward pressure to flex the bristles and "squeeze" the paint out of the brush. And perhaps most important, use as few strokes as possible in order to minimize brush marks. This is especially true on flat, smooth surfaces.

Cleaning Painting Tools

In all cases, rinse brushes thoroughly and comb the bristles with a paint-cleaner tool.

Latex Paint

A solution of water and dish soap is all you need to clean your brushes or rollers, your hands or areas where you may have dripped or spilled latex paint. Use a paint-cleaner tool to squeeze out all of the paint and water from the roller. Rinse thoroughly and hang roller sleeves to dry.

Oil-based Paint

You will need to use either Varsol™, mineral spirits (paint thinner) or lacquer thinner to clean your brushes and hands. It may cost more in time and money to clean a roller sleeve than to purchase another one. However, you can use the roller from one day to the next by first squeezing out as much paint as possible. Leave the sleeve on the roller but wrap it in cellophane. Secure the cellophane with a rubber band and submerge the sleeve in a bucket of water. Find somewhere to spin off any water before reusing sleeve.

Hiding Oil Paint Drips

Trying to clean a drip of oil paint off sidewalks and other rough surfaces sometimes only spreads it out and makes it more obvious. Instead, you can hide the drip by simply wiping a little dirt into the drip area.

Safe Handling & Disposal of Thinners

Mineral spirits and lacquer thinner are highly flammable and toxic materials that should be taken to a hazardous waste recovery facility when no longer in use. Be sure to limit your exposure to these liquids, using in well-ventilated areas. Wash your hands thoroughly after each use.

Boxing is a method by which cans of paint are mixed together in a large bucket to ensure uniformity in colour. Stir thoroughly (possibly using a paint-stirring attachment on your power drill) and then pour the mixed paint back into the original cans if painting with a brush. If you are doing a rolling project, leave the mixed paint in the larger container.

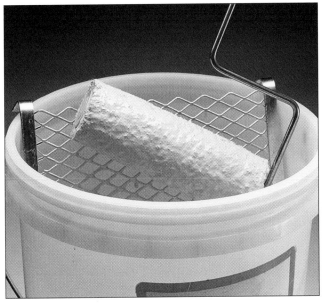

Use a roller screen inside a five-gallon bucket when painting with a roller. Before starting, wet the roller nap with water (if using latex paint), then squeeze out any excess water. Dip the roller in the paint and roll back and forth across the roller screen. The roller sleeve should be full but not dripping when lifted from the container.

Applying Primer & Paint

Be sure to first prime all surfaces to be painted and allow ample drying time before applying the finish coat. These times can vary, depending on the type and brand of the primer. Follow the directions on the label of the can.

How To Paint Exterior Surfaces

1 Paint the face of the fascia first, then cut in paint at the bottom edges of soffit panels. Note that fascia and soffits are usually painted the same colour as the trim. Paint eavestroughs and downspouts after painting the fascia, beginning with the back sides and working toward the front. If you use metal primer, you can paint eaves-troughs and downspouts with trim paint.

2 Paint the soffit panels and trim with a 4" paintbrush. Start by cutting in around the edges of the panels using the narrow edge of the brush, then feather in the broad surfaces of the soffit panels with full loads of paint. Make sure to get good coverage in the groove areas.

3 Paint the bottom edges of lap siding with the paint-brush held flat against the wall. Paint the bottom edges of several siding pieces before returning to paint the faces of the siding boards.

4 Paint broad siding board faces with a 4" brush. Working from the top, paint only as much as you can comfortably reach.

5 Paint all the siding all the way down to the foundation, working from top to bottom. Shift the ladder or scaffolding, and paint the next section. Paint up to the edges of end caps and window

Paint any decorative trim near the top the house at the same time you paint so and fascia. Use a 2½" or 3" paintbrush broader surfaces and a sash brush whe doing more intricate trim work.

and door trim that will be painted later. If trim will not be painted, mask it off or use a paint shield.

6 Paint the foundation with anti-chalking masonry primer. Start by cutting in areas around basement windows. Then, paint the broad surfaces of the foundation with a 4" brush, working the paint into mortar lines.

7 Paint doors and windows using a sash brush. First, paint bevelled edges of raised door panels and the insides of the muntins of window frames. Next, paint door panel faces before the edges dry. Follow this by painting the rails, the horizontal framing members on doors and windows. Finally, do faces of the stiles (photo above).

8 Use a trim or sash brush and a moderate load of paint to cover the inside edges of door and window jambs, casings and brick moulding. Make note that the surfaces on the interior side of the door stop usually match the colour of the interior trim.

9 Paint the outside edges of casings and brick moulding using a sash brush. Mask off freshly painted siding after it has dried.

10 Paint the faces of door jambs, casings and brick moulding, feathering fresh paint around the painted edges.

11 Paint wooden door thresholds and porch floors. Use specially formulated enamel floor paint for maximum durability.

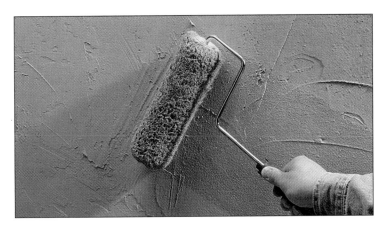

Note these variations: *On stucco siding (photo above), paint the walls with a paint roller and a ⁵/₈" nap sleeve. Use a 3" trim roller or a 3" paintbrush for trim. On board-and-batten or any vertical-panel siding, paint the edges of the battens or top boards first. Paint the faces of the battens before the sides dry, then paint the large, broad surfaces between the battens. Feather in at the edges of the battens. Rollers are good tools for panel siding (use a ⁵/₈" nap sleeve for rough-textured panels).*

BRICK & BLOCK CARE & REPAIR

Brick and mortar reign as kings among building materials due to their strength and durability. But when they are combined in a permanent structure, stress and the forces of nature can lead to damage that requires attention. Common examples of brick and block structural problems include walls with failing mortar joints, cracked or crumbling bricks or blocks, and worn or discoloured surfaces.

Many common brick and block problems can be corrected with simple repairs. These require just a few basic masonry tools and a minimal investment of time and money. The completed repair job will result in a dramatic improvement in the appearance and strength of the structure. With regular maintenance and cleaning, the repaired structure will provide many years of productive use.

Brick and block are used frequently in the construction of foundation walls, retaining walls and other load-bearing structures. Some simple repairs like filling cracks can be done with a low level of risk. But always get a professional evaluation from a masonry contractor before you attempt to make any major repairs to structures of this type.

Choose the best materials and techniques for brick and block structure repairs. A simple chip or popout like the one shown above can be fixed easily by packing the damaged area with latex-fortified mortar. More extensive problems require more complicated solutions.

Tools for Repairing Brick & Block Structures

Basic tools for repairing brick and block include: *a masonry chisel (A) for cutting new brick or block; a stone chisel (B) for breaking up and repairing masonry structures; a raking tool (C) for cleaning mortar out of joints; a mason's trowel (D) for applying mortar to concrete block; a pointing trowel (E) for applying mortar to brick or block, and for smoothing out fresh repairs; a bricklayer's hammer (F); a 1/2" wide (G) and a 3/8" wide (H) joint filler for packing fresh mortar into joints; and a V-shaped mortar tool (I) for finishing mortar joints.*

Identifying Brick & Block Problems

There are usually telltale signs of causes behind brick and block problems, so carefully inspect damaged structures before starting a repair project.

Look for obvious clues like overgrown tree roots or damaged eavestroughs that let water drain onto masonry surfaces. Check, too, to see if the slope of the adjacent landscape is in need of regrading in order to direct water away from a block or brick wall. In some cases, consult with a landscape architect.

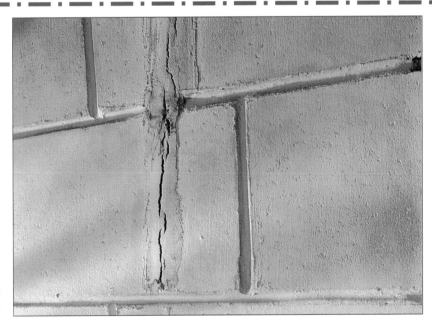

Repairs fail *when the original source of the problem is not eliminated prior to making the repair. When a concrete patch separates, for example, it means that the opposing stresses causing the crack are still at work on the structure. Problems such as this are often attributed to a failing sub-base, stress from water, or freezing and thawing.*

Common Problems

Deteriorated Mortar Joints. Because mortar is softer than most bricks or blocks, it is more prone to damage and is a common source of problems. Deterioration is not always visible, so probe surrounding joints with a screwdriver to see if they are sound. Tuckpoint (repair with fresh mortar) deteriorated joints.

Major Structural Damage. This usually requires removal of the existing structure, sub-base improvements and reconstruction of the structure. This is a job for a professional mason.

Damage to Concrete Blocks. Repeated freezing and thawing of moisture in a wall or in blocks often is the cause of such a problem. Instead of replacing the whole block, repair the damaged concrete block or blocks by chipping out the face of the block and replacing it with a concrete paver with the same dimensions as the block face.

Stains and Discolouration. Look for external sources as causes of this problem, or minerals leaching to the surface from within the brick or block (called efflorescence). If the stain does not wash away easily with water, use a cleaning solution.

Damaged Mortar Chimney Caps. This problem allows water to enter the flue area of the chimney, where it can damage the chimney itself or even the roof or interior walls. Small-scale damage can be patched with fire-rated silicone caulk. If damage is extensive, repair or replace the mortar cap.

Spalling occurs when freezing water or other forces cause enough directional pressure to fracture a brick. The best solution is to replace the entire brick while eliminating the source of the pressure, if possible. Spalled blocks can be refaced. When looking for a replacement, chip off a piece of the damaged brick to use as a colour reference.

Preparing & Replacing Mortar

When making mortar repairs, add concrete fortifier to increase the overall strength and bondability of mortar. Fortifiers are either acrylic- or latex-based.

Add mortar pigment to plain mortar so repairs blend in better. To match mortar colours, compare pigment samples from concrete product suppliers.

Repairing Brick & Block Walls

Brick and block walls deteriorate quickly once a crack or fissure has formed. The most common brick and block wall repair technique is tuckpointing – the process of replacing failed mortar joints with fresh mortar. Tuckpointing is a highly useful repair technique for any homeowner. It can be used to repair walls, chimneys, brick veneer or any other structure where the bricks or blocks are bonded with mortar.

Minor cosmetic repairs can be attempted on any type of wall – from free-standing garden walls to block foundations. Filling minor cracks with caulk or repair compound, patching pop-outs or chips and replacing individual bricks are good examples. Consult a professional before attempting any major repairs like replacing a large area of brick or blocks.

Basement walls are a frequent trouble area for homeowners. Constant moisture and stress created by ground contact can cause leaks, bowing and paint failure. Small leaks and cracks can be patched with hydraulic cement. Masonry-based waterproofing products can be applied to give the deteriorated walls a fresh appearance. Persistent moisture problems are most often caused by improper grading of soil around the foundation or a malfunctioning eavestrough system.

> **TIP:**
>
> Be sure to save fragments for use as a colour reference when you shop for replacement bricks.

Make timely repairs to brick and block structures. *Tuckpointing deteriorated mortar joints (photos above) is a common repair that, like other types of repairs, improves the appearance of the structure or surface and helps prevent further damage.*

How to Tuckpoint Mortar Joints

1 Clean out loose or deteriorated mortar to a depth of 1/4" to 3/4". Use a mortar raking tool first, then switch to a masonry chisel and a hammer if necessary. Clear away all loose debris and dampen the surface with water before applying fresh mortar.

2 Mix the mortar, adding concrete fortifier. If joints have discoloured, add pigment. Push mortar into the horizontal joints with a joint filler. Apply mortar in 1/4"-thick layers and allow 30 minutes of drying between layers. Fill the joints until the mortar is flush with the face of the brick or block.

3 Apply the first layer of mortar into the vertical joints by scooping mortar onto the back of a joint filler and pressing it into the joint. Work from the top, downward.

4 After the final layer of mortar is applied, smooth the joints with a jointing tool that matches the profile of the old mortar joints. Tool the horizontal joints first. Let the mortar dry until it is crumbly, then brush off the excess mortar with a stiff-bristled brush.

How to Replace a Damaged Brick

1 Score the damaged brick so it will break more easily for removal. Use a power drill with a masonry-cutting disc to score lines along the surface of the brick and in the mortar joints surrounding the brick.

2 Use a mason's chisel and hammer to break apart the damaged brick along the scored lines. Rap sharply on the chisel, taking care to not damage surrounding bricks.

3 Chisel out remaining mortar in the cavity, then brush out debris with a stiff-bristled or wire brush to create a clean surface. Rinse the repair area surface with water.

4 Mix the mortar for the repair, adding concrete fortifier to the mixture and pigment if needed to match the old mortar. Apply a 1"-thick layer of mortar to the bottom and sides of the wall cavity.

Use a mortar hawk (above, top) *for keeping mortar in close proximity while doing tuckpointing work. Use a pointing trowel* (above, bottom) *to apply the mortar in the bottom and sides of the wall cavity.*

RECOMMENDED POWER TOOLS

MASTERCRAFT

DRILL

NEEDED MATERIALS

- mortar
- concrete fortifier
- pigment
- concrete paver

RECOMMENDED HAND TOOLS

- basic hand tools
- raking tool
- chisel
- joint filler
- pointing trowel
- jointing tool
- wire brush
- masonry drill bit
- masonry cutting disc
- mortar hawk

5 Dampen the replacement brick slightly, then apply mortar to brick ends and top. Fit the brick into the cavity and rap with the trowel handle until the face is flush with surrounding bricks. If needed, press more mortar into joints with a pointing trowel.

6 Scrape away excess mortar, then smooth the joints with a jointing tool that matches the profile of the surrounding mortar joints. Let the mortar set until crumbly, then brush the joints to remove excess mortar.

How To Reinforce Refaced Block Sections

1 Reinforce repair areas with two or more adjacent block faces. Start by drilling a few holes in a small area over a core in the block located directly above the repair area. Chip out the block face between the holes with a cold chisel.

2 Prepare a thin mortar mix made from one part dry gravel and two parts dry mortar. Add water. The mixture should be thin enough to pour easily but not so it has a soupy consistency. If you want to increase the amount and strength of the mortar you are using, add some gravel to the mix.

3 Pour the mortar and gravel mixture into the hole above the repair area using a piece of metal flashing as a funnel. Continue mixing and filling the hole until it will not accept any more mortar. The mortar will dry to form a reinforcing column that is bonded to the backs of the pavers used to reface the blocks.

4 Patch the hole above the repair area by using a pointing trowel to fill the hole with plain mortar mix. Smooth the surface with the pointing trowel, then finish the joint below the patch using your jointing tool.

Special Circumstances

For walls with extensive damage, remove bricks from the top down, one row at a time. Leave dismantling of load-bearing brick structures like foundation walls to a professional mason.

For walls with internal damage, remove only the damaged section. Keep upper layers intact if they are sound. Do not remove more than four adjacent blocks in one area without temporary support.

How To Reface Damaged Concrete Block

1 Drill several holes into the face of the deteriorated block at the cores (hollow spots) of the block using a masonry bit. Wear protective eye covering.

2 Using the holes as starters, chip away block face with a chisel and hammer.

3 Use a cold chisel to chip out a 2"-deep recess in the web areas (photo below). Mark and score cutting lines 2" back from the block face, then chisel out the block in the recess area. Leave enough for a bonding surface for the concrete paver.

4 Mix mortar and apply a 1"-thick layer to the sides, bottom and the webs, and top edge and webs on the paver. Press the paver into the cavity, flush with surrounding blocks. Add mortar to joint if needed, finish joints with a jointing tool and prop a 2x4 against the paver until the mortar sets.

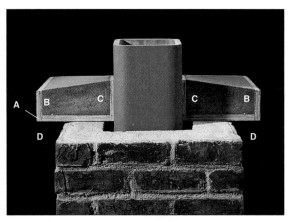

Put an end to annual trips up to the roof to fix a cracked mortar cap by building and installing a "floating" chimney cap. A floating chimney cap (photo left) is cast in a form using mortar- or sand-mix concrete. It is then placed on the top of the chimney. It is not permanently bonded to the chimney or flue, so it can move independently as the chimney temperature changes. The mortar cap, constructed of 3/4"-thick plywood (A), is shown cutaway. The vertical dimensions of the cap are 3½" on the outside edge (B) by 4¾" on the edge next to the flue (C). There is a 2" overhang on all sides (D).

Chimney Repair

How to Cast & Install a Chimney Cap

1 Measure the chimney and flue and build a form from 3/4"-thick plywood (see dimensions above). Attach the form to a plywood base, using 1½" wood screws to connect form parts. Make a frame from 3/8" dowels, 1" inside the form. Glue the dowel frame to the form base to cast a drip edge into the cap.

2 Prepare a stiff (dry) mixture of mortar. For an average-size chimney, two 60-pound bags of dry mix should yield enough. Fill the form with mortar. Rest a wood float across the edges of the form and strike off the mortar. Keep angles

sharp at the corners. Let the cap cure for at least two days, then carefully disassemble the form.

3 Chip off old mortar cap and clean top of chimney with a wire brush. With a helper, transport the cap onto the roof and set it directly onto the chimney, centred so the overhang is equal on all sides. Do not bond it to chimney or flue.

4 Shift cap so the gap next to flue is even on all sides, then fill it with fire-rated rope or mineral wool. Caulk over the fill material with a heavy bead of fire-rated silicone caulk. Caulk joint at underside of cap. Inspect caulk bi-annually.

How To Repair Chimney Caps

1 Carefully break apart and remove deteriorated sections of the chimney cap, using a cold chisel and hammer. Be careful around the flue.

2 Mix a batch of latex-fortified mortar. Trowel an even layer of mortar around the chimney cap, following the slope of the existing cap. Mortar should cover chimney from outside edges of chimney bricks to the flue. Smooth out mortar with a wood float, re-creating the original slope of the chimney cap. Inspect annually.

RECOMMENDED POWER TOOLS

MASTERCRAFT

DRILL

RECOMMENDED HAND TOOLS

- basic hand tools
- cold chisel
- wood float
- pointing trowel

NEEDED MATERIALS

- 3/4"-thick plywood for form construction
- 1/4" dowel
- 1½" wood screws
- fire-rated silicone caulk
- 3/8" dowels
- latex fortified mortar
- glue
- fire-rated rope or mineral wool

Cleaning & Painting Brick & Block

The key to keeping brick and block surface stains and discolouration problems from becoming permanent is to treat them quickly. Check your brick and block surfaces as part of your annual house inspection, using the information below to address specific problems.

Painted brick and block structures can be spruced up by applying a fresh coat of paint. As with any other painting job, thorough surface preparation and use of quality primer are critical to a successful outcome.

Regular maintenance will keep brick and block structures looking their best.

Use a pressure washer *to clean large brick and block structures.*

Solvent Solutions for Common Brick & Block Stains

- ❏ **Egg splatter:** Dissolve oxalic acid crystals in water in a non-metallic container, following manufacturer's instructions.
- ❏ **Efflorescence:** Scrub surface with a stiff-bristled brush. Use a household cleaning solution for surfaces with heavy accumulation.
- ❏ **Iron stains:** Spray or brush a solution of oxalic acid crystals dissolved in water, following manufacturer's instructions. Apply directly to the stain.
- ❏ **Ivy:** Cut vines away from the surface. (Do not pull them off.) Let remaining stems dry up, then scrub them off with a stiff-bristled brush and household cleaning solution.

- ❏ **Oil:** Apply a paste made of mineral spirits and an inert material like sawdust.
- ❏ **Paint stains:** Remove new paint with a solution of TSP (trisodium phosphate) and water, following mixing instructions on the label. Old paint can usually be removed with heavy scrubbing or sand-blasting.
- ❏ **Plant growth:** Use weed killer according to directions.
- ❏ **Smoke stains:** Scrub surface with household cleanser containing bleach or use a mixture of ammonia and water.

Making Brick & Block Cleaning Paste

You can easily mix a brick and block cleaning paste using cleaning solvents (as suggested on the previous page) and talcum or flour. Apply the paste directly to the stain (photo left), let it dry and then scrape it off with a vinyl or plastic scraper (do not use a metal scraper on brick, block or masonry surfaces). Use a nylon scraper or a thin block of wood to clean up spilled, hardened mortar.

TIP:

Mask off windows, siding, decorative millwork and other exposed non-masonry surfaces before cleaning brick and block. Careful masking is essential if you are using harsh cleaning chemicals like muriatic acid solutions.

Cleaning & Painting Masonry

When cleaning masonry, always test cleaning solutions on a small area of the surface to evaluate the results. Some chemicals and their fumes may be harmful. Be sure to follow manufacturer's safety and use recommendations. Wear protective clothing.

Soak the surface with water before applying solutions. Thoroughly rinse off any remaining solution.

Clean mortar joints using a drill with a wire wheel attachment. Scrub off loose paint, dirt and mineral deposits so the paint will bond better.

Apply masonry primer before repainting brick or block walls (photo right). Primer helps to eliminate stains and prevent problems like efflorescence.

CONCRETE CARE & REPAIR

Good repairs restore both the appearance and the function of failing concrete structures and surfaces. Careful work can produce a well-blended, successful repair, like the one shown before (above top) and after (above bottom).

Concrete is known for its durability, strength and ability to be shaped and moulded to meet a wide range of applications. These same attributes can be applied to concrete repairs, if they are properly carried out.

Problems with concrete can often be traced to improper finishing techniques, a poor sub-base, lack of reinforcement, or freezing and thawing before drying is complete. By addressing problems as soon as possible and correcting their possible causes before doing concrete repairs, you can prevent further or recurring damage.

Concrete repair projects fall into a wide range – from simple cleaning and sealing, to completely removing and replacing whole sections. Filling cracks and repairing surface damage are the most common repairs. Another effective repair is resurfacing or covering an old concrete surface with fresh concrete. It is a good option for spalling, crazing or pop-outs – minor problems that affect the appearance more than the structure.

As with any kind of repair, the success of the project depends largely on good preparation and using the best products for the job. Specially formulated repair products are made for just about every type of concrete repair. Before purchasing one, read the product-use information and note if it needs to be used with any other product.

A good repair can outlast the rest of the structure in some cases, but if structural damage has occurred, repairing the concrete is only a temporary solution. By using the right products and techniques, you can make cosmetic repairs that improve the appearance of the surface and keep damage from getting worse.

Concrete Repair Products

Concrete repair products include: vinyl-reinforced concrete patch (A) for filling holes, pop-outs and larger cracks; hydraulic cement (B) for repairing foundations, retaining walls and other damp areas; quick-setting cement (C) for repairing vertical surfaces and unusual shapes; anchoring cement (D) for setting hardware in concrete; concrete sealing products (E); concrete recoating product (F) for creating a fresh surface on old concrete; masonry paint (G); joint-filler caulk (H); pour-in crack sealer (I); concrete cleaner (J); concrete fortifier (K) to strengthen concrete; bonding adhesive (L) to prepare the repair area; and concrete sand mix (M) for general repairs and resurfacing.

Tips for Disguising Repairs

To create a colour that matches the original concrete, add concrete pigment to concrete patching compound. Experiment with different mixtures of pigment and repair cement until you find the right mixture. Samples should be dry to show the actual colours.

To cover concrete repairs, use masonry paint (photo right). Paint can be used on vertical or horizontal surfaces. High-traffic surfaces will require more frequent touch-up or repainting.

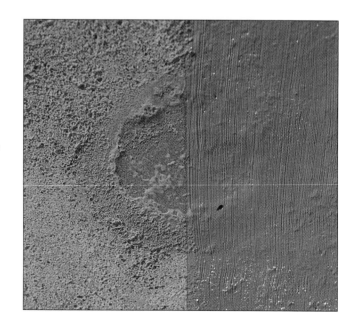

Common Concrete Problems

❑ **Crazing** – widespread cracks all the way through the surface, and other forms of substantial damage, are very difficult to repair effectively. If the damage to the concrete is extensive, remove and replace the entire structure.

❑ **Frost** heave is common in colder climates. Frozen ground forces concrete slabs upward, and sections of the slab can pop up. The best solution is to break off and remove the affected section or sections, repair the sub-base and pour new sections that are set off by isolation joints.

❑ **Sunken concrete** usually is caused by erosion of the sub-base. Some structures like sidewalks can be raised to repair the sub-base, then relaid. A more common and more reliable solution is to hire a mud-jacking contractor to raise the surface by injecting fresh concrete below it.

❑ **Moisture buildup** occurs in concrete structures like foundations and retaining walls, which are in constant contact with the ground. To identify the moisture source, tape a piece of foil to the wall. If moisture collects on the outer surface of the foil, the probable cause is condensation. If moisture is not visible on the foil, it could be seeping through the wall. Consult a professional mason.

❑ **Staining** can ruin the appearance of a concrete surface or structure. Stains can be removed with commercial-grade concrete cleaner or other chemicals. To avoid staining, seal surfaces with a clear sealant.

❑ **Isolated cracks** occur on many concrete building projects. Fill small cracks with concrete caulk or crack filler. Patch large cracks with vinyl-reinforced patching material.

❑ **Pop-outs** can be caused by freezing moisture or stress, but very often they occur because the concrete surface was improperly floated or cured. This causes the aggregate near the surface of the concrete to loosen. A few scattered pop-outs do not require attention unless they are very large or widespread. In this case, repair them as you would repair holes.

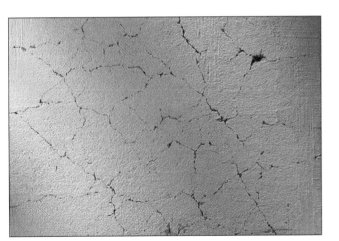

Crazing is widespread hairline cracks, usually caused by overfloating, which draws too much water to the surface. Clean and seal the surface to help prevent further crazing. For a long-term solution, resurface.

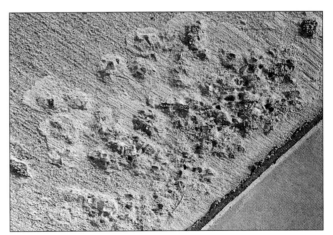

Spalling is surface deterioration of concrete. It is caused by overfloating. This weakens the surface and causes it to peel off over time. When spalling occurs, it is usually widespread and cause for resurfacing.

RECOMMENDED HAND TOOLS

- basic hand tools
- wire brush
- wire wheel attachment for drill
- stone chisel
- hand maul
- paintbrush
- trowel

NEEDED MATERIALS

- mortar
- concrete fortifier
- pigment
- concrete bonding adhesive

TIP:
Bonding adhesive, vinyl-reinforced patching compound, and fortifier products for concrete will improve the quality of your work and make the repairs long-lasting. They are more than worth the relatively small extra expense.

Filling Cracks

Consider the location and size of a crack when determining which materials and methods you will use for repairs. For small cracks (less than ¼" wide), you can use grey-tinted concrete caulk for a quick fix (see pages 10-11). For more permanent solutions, use pourable crack filler or fortified patching cements. The patching cements are polymer compounds that significantly increase the bonding properties of cement and allow some flexibility.

Cracked Concrete Repair Preparation

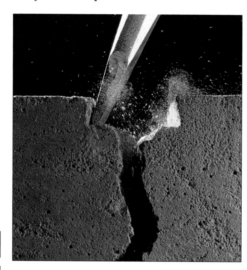

To prepare the crack for repair work, clean out loose material with a wire brush or a portable drill with a wire wheel attachment. Loose material or debris left in the crack will result in a poor bond and an ineffective repair. Next, chisel out the crack. Using a stone chisel, hammer and a pair of safety goggles, create a backward-angled cut that is wider at the base than at the surface (photo above). The angled cut-out

shape prevents the repair material from pushing out of the crack.

For larger cracks on flat surfaces, use fortified sand-mix concrete. To fill cracks on vertical surfaces, use hydraulic or quick-setting cement. Thorough preparation of the cracked surface is essential for creating a good bonding surface.

How to Repair Small Cracks

1 After preparing a crack for repair, apply a thin layer of bonding adhesive to the entire repair area using a paintbrush. The bonding adhesive helps keep repair material from loosening or popping out.

2 Next, mix a batch of vinyl-reinforced patching compound and then trowel it into the crack (photo below). Gradually taper off the amount of compound applied by "feathering" it so it is even with the surrounding surface.

Variations for Repairing Large Cracks

Horizontal Surfaces: Prepare the crack as discussed on the preceding page, then pour sand into the crack to within ½" of the surface. Prepare sand-mix concrete by adding a concrete fortifier, then trowel the mixture into the crack. Using a trowel, feather the mixture until it is even with the surface.

Vertical Surfaces: Prepare the crack and then mix a batch of vinyl-reinforced concrete or hydraulic cement. Trowel a ¼"- to ½"-thick layer into the crack until the crack is slightly over-filled. Let it dry and then feather edges even with the surface. If the crack is deep (over ½" thick), trowel in more layers, allowing drying time between each layer.

Patching Holes

You will find that large and small holes are treated differently when it comes to concrete repairs. The best product for filling in smaller holes (less than ½" deep) is vinyl-reinforced concrete patcher. Because reinforced repair products should be applied only in layers that are ½" thick or less, use a sand-mix concrete with an acrylic or latex fortifier for holes more than a ½" deep. Sand mix can be applied in layers up to 2" thick.

The location of a hole also can play a part in your product selection. Use hydraulic or quick-setting cement for repairing holes and chip-outs in vertical surfaces. Because they set up in just a few minutes, these products can be shaped to fill holes without the need for forms. If the structure is exposed constantly to moisture, use hydraulic cement. Patches in concrete will be more effective if you create clean, backward-angled cuts (as previously discussed) around the damaged area. This improves bonding. Use masonry blades for cutting concrete.

Preparing Holes for Repair

For small holes, cut out around the damaged area with a masonry-grinding disc mounted on a portable drill, or use a hammer and stone chisel. The cuts should bevel about 15° away from the centre of the damaged area. Chisel out any loose concrete within the repair area. Always wear gloves and eye protection.

For large holes, mark straight cutting lines around the damaged area. Then, cut with a circular saw equipped with a masonry-cutting blade (photo right). Adjust the foot of the saw so the cut bevels away from the damage at a 15° angle. Set the foot of the saw on a thin board to protect it from the concrete. Chisel out any remaining concrete within the repair area.

Repairing Small Holes

Prepare the damaged area as described on previous pages, then apply a thin layer of bonding adhesive to help create a sturdy bond with the patch.

Fill the damaged area with vinyl-reinforced patching compound, applied in layers no thicker than ¼" to ½". Add layers of patching mixture until the hole is filled just above the surface level, allowing about 30 minutes between coats. Feather out the surface and let the repair cure.

Resurfacing Concrete

In some cases, you may have concrete that has surface damage but is still structurally sound. Preserve these areas by resurfacing, which involves applying a thin layer of new concrete over the old surface. If the old surface has deep cracks or extensive damage, resurfacing will only temporarily solve the problem. A bonding agent helps the new surface adhere to the old. Because new concrete will bond to the old surface better if it is packed down, use a dry, stiff concrete mixture that can be compacted with a shovel.

Repairing Large Holes

After preparing the damaged area as described earlier, mix sand-mix concrete with concrete acrylic fortifier and fill the damaged area slightly above the surrounding surface.

Smooth out and feather the repair with a wood float until the repair is level with the surrounding surface. Re-create any surface finish (by whisk-brooming the surface or other such means) that was used on the original surface.

Resurface concrete that has extensive surface damage like spalling or pop-outs. Because the new surface is so thin (1" to 2"), use sand-mix concrete. If you are having ready-mix concrete delivered by a concrete contractor, make sure they do not use aggregate larger than ½" in the mixture.

Resurfacing Concrete

1 Clean the surface thoroughly. If the surface is flaking or spalled, scrape it with a spade to dislodge as much loose concrete as you can, then sweep the surface clean.

2 Dig a 6"-wide trench around the surface on all sides for 2x4 forms.

3 Stake 2x4 forms flush against the sides of the concrete slabs, 1" to 2" above the surface (make sure height is even). Drive stakes every three feet and at every joint in forms. Mark control joint locations onto the outside of the forms, directly above existing control joints. Coat inside edges of the forms with vegetable oil.

4 Apply a thin layer of bonding adhesive over the entire surface. Follow the directions on the bonding product container.

5 Mix sand-mix concrete, slightly stiffer (drier) than normal concrete. Spread the concrete, then press down on it with a shovel or 2x4 to pack the mixture into the forms. Smooth the surface with a screed board.

6 Float the concrete with a wood float, then tool with an edger. Re-create any surface treatment, such as brooming, used on the original surface. Cut control joints in the original locations. Let the surface cure for one week, covered with plastic.

Repairing Steps

Steps require more repairs than other concrete structures because of heavy use. Horizontal surfaces can be treated using the same products and techniques used on other masonry surfaces. For vertical areas, use quick-setting cement and shape it to fit.

Replacing a Step Corner

First, retrieve the broken corner, then clean it and the mating surface using a wire brush. Apply bonding adhesive to both surfaces. Rebuild the corner with quick-setting cement if you don't have the piece.

Spread a heavy layer of fortified patching cement on the surfaces to be joined, then press the piece into position (photo right). Lean a brick or block against the repair until the compound sets, and protect from use for one week.

How To Patch Step Treads

1 Make a cut in the stair tread just outside the damaged area, using a circular saw with a masonry cutting blade. Make the cut so it angles toward the back of the step. Make a similar cut on the riser below the damaged area, then chisel out the area in between the two cuts.

2 Cut a form board the same height as the step riser. Press it against the riser of the damaged step and brace it in position with heavy blocks. Make sure the top of the form is flush with the top of the step tread.

3 Apply bonding adhesive to the repair area, then press a stiff mixture of quick-setting cement into the damaged area with a trowel.

4 Smooth off the concrete with a wood float and let it set for a few minutes. Round over the front edge of the nose with an edger. Use a trowel to slice off the sides of the patch so it is flush with the side of the steps. Wait at least overnight before allowing traffic on the step.

Miscellaneous Concrete Repairs

There are plenty of concrete problems you may encounter around your house that are not always addressed in repair manuals. These include tasks such as resetting posts and post anchors; patching contoured objects that have been damaged; and repairing masonry veneer around the foundation of your house. You can adapt basic concrete repair techniques to make just about any type of concrete repair.

How to Repair Shaped Concrete

1 Scrape all loose material and debris from the damaged area, then wipe down with water. Mix and trowel quick-setting cement into the area. Work quickly – you only have a few minutes before the concrete sets up.

2 Use the trowel or putty knife to mould concrete to follow the form of the object being repaired. Smooth the concrete as soon as it sets up. Buff with emery paper to smooth out ridges after the repair dries.

Reset loose masonry anchors by removing the anchors and filling the old holes with anchoring cement. Then, press the anchors into the fresh cement. Anchoring cement expands as it dries, creating a tighter repair. Make sure the anchors are not disturbed while the cement sets up (usually within about an hour).

How to Repair Masonry Veneer

1 Chip off the crumbled, loose or deteriorated veneer from the wall using a cold chisel and hammer. Chisel away damaged veneer until you have only a good, solid surface remaining. Use care to avoid damaging the wall behind the veneer. Clean the repair area with a wire brush.

2 Clean up any metal lath in the repair area if it is in good condition. If not, cut it out with aviator snips. Add new lath where needed, using masonry anchors to hold it to the wall.

3 Mix fortified sand-mix concrete (or specialty concrete blends for wall repair) and trowel it over the lath until it is even with the surrounding surfaces.

4 Re-create the surface texture to match the surrounding area. You may want to use a stiff-bristled brush, for example, to stipple the surface. You can also blend in the repair by adding pigment to the sand mixture, or paint the repair area after it dries.

Sealing & Maintaining Concrete

Protect concrete that is exposed to heavy traffic or constant moisture by sealing it with a clear concrete sealer. Options include:

Exposed-aggregate Sealer. Applied about three weeks after concrete is poured, this keeps aggregate from loosening. It should be applied with a roller after washing the surface and allowing it to dry.

Clear Concrete Sealer. Meant as a clear, water-resistant seal on the surface, this is acrylic based, does not attract dirt and can help concrete cure evenly.

Masonry Recoating. Applied like paint, this will look like fresh concrete when dry. It will improve the appearance of walls but generally have little waterproofing value.

Specially formulated concrete paints help keep minerals in the concrete from leaching through paint and hardening into a white, dusty film or efflorescence. They are sold in many stock colours or can be custom mixed.

Regular cleaning also helps prevent deterioration from oils and de-icing salts. Use concrete cleaner products for scheduled cleanings and special solutions for specific types of stains.

TIP:
Clean oil stains on concrete by dampening sawdust with paint thinner, then applying the sawdust over the stain (photo left). The paint thinner will break apart the stain, allowing the oil to be absorbed by the sawdust. Wipe up with a broom when finished and reapply as necessary. You also can fill the dividing lines or control joints in concrete with concrete repair caulk. This keeps water from accumulating and damaging the concrete.

TIP:
Your home may have an area where a hard surface like a concrete walkway runs up against the foundation. The crack between these surfaces is a natural place for rainwater to enter your home and cause water problems in the basement. In these cases, run a heavy bead of caulk-type concrete patcher along this open seam. Recheck and repatch these areas every couple of years.

How to Patch Pop-ups & Cracks in Concrete

1 Chip out rocks at bottom of pop-up hole with a masonry chisel and hammer. Wear goggles to avoid eye injury.

2 Remove dirt and debris from the hole with a shop vacuum. If the hole contains oil or grease, wash it with detergent, then rinse with water.

3 Coat the edges of the hole with a latex bonding liquid. Mix concrete with water, then stir in the liquid. Pour in the mixture and smooth with a flexible knife or trowel.

Asphalt Care & Repair

Impact or water penetration are the two key contributors to the breakdown of asphalt blacktop driveways. Water running under blacktop from the side or through cracks undermines the gravel base cushioning the slab. To prevent serious damage, fill holes and cracks with asphalt patcher, seal the surface and fill washouts along the slab edge to prevent water from entering.

How to Patch Holes in Asphalt

1 Remove dirt and debris from the hole with a shop vacuum. Flush the hole with a garden hose and spray nozzle.

2 Pour asphalt patching material into the hole. Warm the patch material with a heat gun (photo below). Level and smooth the patch with a trowel.

3 Tamp patching material so it is firmly packed in the hole. Firm, smooth patches prevent future water damage.

Sealing an Asphalt Drive

Seal-coating your asphalt driveway not only improves its overall appearance but can also help provide some level of preventative maintenance.

TIP:

For best results use acrylic driveway products, like sealer and patcher, warranted not to peel or flake for three years.

How to Seal an Asphalt Drive

1 When starting an asphalt drive sealing project, first fill any holes as described in the previous section. Clean the slab with an asphalt cleaning product to remove oil and dirt from the surface. Rinse the slab with a hose or power washer.

2 Patch cracks in asphalt using a caulk gun and a tube of asphalt patcher (photo below). Large cracks may need several applications.

3 Spread and smooth out the patch material with a putty knife (photo right). Dip the knife in cold water or thinner to prevent sticking.

4 Pour a pool of sealer on the slab and spread it, following manufacturer's directions. Too thin of a layer will not cure properly. It is better to apply two coats.

5 Allow the sealer to cure before driving or walking on it. Block the driveway with sawhorses or rope and ladders to prevent traffic during the drying period.

REPAIRING EAVESTROUGHS

Rehanging sagging eavestroughs *is a common eavestrough repair. Before rehanging them, snap a chalk line that follows the original slope (usually about 1/4" per 10' toward the downspouts). To rehang eavestroughs, remove the hangers in and near the sag, and lift the eavestrough until it is flush with the chalk line. Reattach the hangers (or replace them if they are in bad condition), shifting their location slightly so you do not use the original holes. If the hangers are more than 24" apart or there is no hanger within 12" of a seam, add hangers.*

Eavestroughs channel water away from your home. Clogged, sagging or leaky eavestroughs can cause extensive damage to your siding, foundation or landscaping. They can also be a key contributor to a wet basement.

Evaluate the type and extent of eavestrough damage when determining the best repair method. Often, small leaks and minor damage can be repaired with easy-to-use eavestrough repair products. Moderate damage to metal eavestroughs can be patched with flashing. To prevent corrosion, be sure to patch with the same type of metal (usually aluminum or galvanized steel) from which the eavestroughs are made.

If the damaged area is more than two feet in length, replace the entire section of eavestrough with new material. To locate a replacement section of eavestrough for making repairs, trace the profile of your existing eavestroughs and take it with you when purchasing new materials. Bring along measurements of the eavestrough at its widest point. If your eavestroughs are more than 15 years old, they likely are a little larger than eavestroughs made today. In these cases, check salvage yards or have a new section custom bent by a metal fabricator.

If your eavestroughs are beyond repair, remove and replace them. Snap-together vinyl eavestroughs (page 51) are popular and relatively easy to install.

Some houses even have wooden eavestroughs. In this case, patch small holes or rot with epoxy wood filler. If damage is more serious, contact a professional carpenter.

Tips for Eavestrough Maintenance & Repair

❏ Install eavestrough guards. These prevent the build-up of debris in the eavestroughs. Buy the size and style that match your eavestroughs. Use downspout strainers to prevent debris from collecting in downspouts, where it is harder to remove.

❏ Install a swing-up elbow. Added at the end of each drain pipe, these allow the outlet pipe to be lifted out of the way when you are working near the foundation. Add a splash block, too, to prevent erosion and help direct water away from the house.

❏ Use eavestrough caulk. Small holes and minor leaks can be repaired with these butyl-rubber caulks. They flex without losing their seal and are resistant to the elements.

How to Repair Leaky Joints

1 Drill out rivets or remove metal screws that secure the joint (photo above). Disassemble the damaged joint. With downspouts, you may need to disassemble the entire downspout to get the bad joint apart.

2 Scrub both parts of the joint using a stiff-bristled brush (for vinyl eavestroughs) or a wire brush (for metal eavestroughs). Clean the damaged area with water.

3 When dry, apply caulk to the joining parts, then reassemble the joint. Reinforce the joint with new fasteners. Add new hangers if the originals need replacing.

How to Patch Metal Eavestroughs

1 Clean the area around the damage with a wire brush. Scrub with an abrasive pad to loosen residue, then clean the area with water.

2 Apply a ⅛"-thick layer of roof cement evenly over the damage and spread it a few inches beyond the damaged area on all sides.

3 Cut and bend a patch from flashing made from the same material as the eavestroughs. Bed it in the cement and feather the cement so it won't cause damming.

How to Replace a Section of Metal Eavestrough

1 Remove eavestrough hangers in or near the damaged area. Insert wood spacers in the eavestrough near each hanger (photo above left), before putting pressure on the eavestrough. This helps protect eavestroughs from damage.

2 Slip spacers between the eavestrough and fascia, near each end of the damaged area, so you do not damage the roof when cutting the eavestrough. Cut out the damaged area with a hacksaw.

3 Cut an eavestrough patch from material similar in type, size and profile to the original eavestrough. The patch should be at least 4" longer than the damaged section.

4 With a wire brush, clean the cut ends of the old eavestrough. Caulk the ends, then centre the eavestrough patch over the damage and press into caulk.

5 Secure the eavestrough patch with rivets or sheet-metal screws (photo above right). Use at least three or four fasteners at each joint. On the inside surfaces of the eavestrough, caulk over the heads of the fasteners.

6 Install the eavestrough hangers, using new hangers if necessary. (Do not use the old holes.) Prime and paint the patch to match.

Estimating Eavestrough Parts

- **Sections:** Measure total length of the run; add 15% for waste. Sold in 10' lengths.
- **Hangers:** One for every 2' of eavestrough.
- **Inside/outside corners:** One for every 2'.
- **Connectors:** Two per corner; one per 10' of eaves-trough.
- **End caps (right or left):** One per end.
- **Downspout outlets:** One for every 35' of eavestrough.
- **Downspout elbows:** Three per downspout.
- **Drain pipe:** One pipe per downspout outlet. Measure eavestrough height and add 5' for each pipe (for splice-block outlet and waste). Sold in 10' lengths.
- **Drain pipe hangers:** Two per drain pipe.

Installing a Vinyl Snap-together Eavestrough System

Snap-together eavestrough systems are designed to install easily, requiring no fasteners other than the screws used to attach the eavestrough hangers to the fascia. Draw a detailed plan before purchasing new eavestroughs. See above list on planning and estimating. You may find it helpful to test-fit all the pieces on the ground before you begin the actual installation.

RECOMMENDED POWER TOOLS

MASTERCRAFT

DRILL

How to Install a Vinyl Snap-together Eavestrough System

1 Mark a point at the high end of each eavestrough run, 1" down from the top of the fascia (photo above). Snap chalk lines that slope ¼" per 10' toward downspout outlets. For runs longer than 35', mark a slope from a high point in the centre toward downspouts at each end.

2 Install downspout outlets near the ends of eaves-trough runs (at least one outlet for every 35' of run). The tops of the outlets should be flush with the slope line, and they should align with end caps on your house's corners where drain pipes will be attached (photo above right).

RECOMMENDED HAND TOOLS

- basic hand tools
- chalk line
- hacksaw
- screwdriver bits

NEEDED MATERIALS

- 1¼" deck screws
- eavestroughs and drain pipes
- connectors and fittings

ROOF REPAIRS

It should come as no surprise that your roof system requires the highest degree of maintenance. As your home's highest and most vulnerable point, it is subjected to the hot summer sun, standing snow and ice, high winds and other weather-related elements. The vital role your roof plays in protecting your home underscores the attention required in order to avoid leaks and maintain proper ventilation.

A roof system is composed of several elements that work together to provide three basic and essential functions for your home: shelter, drainage and ventilation. The roof covering and the metal flashing in valleys and around chimneys, vent pipes and other roof elements, seals out and sheds water. It also directs water to eavestroughs and downspouts, which in turn channel water away from the foundation. Air intake and outlet vents keep fresh air circulating below the roof sheathing, preventing moisture build-up and overheating. Soffits cover and protect the eave area below the roof overhang, while fascia supports soffit panels as well as an eavestrough and downspout system.

Whatever the complexity of the repairs required, it is very important that you have a thorough understanding of how all elements of your roof system work. By understanding your system and making timely repairs, you can ensure that your roof system performs for its full, useful lifespan.

Evaluating Roofs

Regular inspections, maintenance and minor roof repairs can minimize the threat of damage to your home due to roof failure. It is a good idea to familiarize yourself with signs of shingle wear, in the form of buckled, curled or cupped shingles, or gravel in downspouts or rain eavestroughs.

While broken shingles and other isolated damage or wear can be remedied by replacing shingles in affected areas, widespread damage may call for a total roof replacement. A second roof layer can be applied on top of another. Do not install new shingles over cupped or buckled roofing.

The first step is to determine the cause of a problem before adding and investing in new materials. Shingle warpage and buckling is often due to condensation from poor attic ventilation or leaky shingles and flashing. Limbs overhanging a roof can cause moss build-up if sunlight can not get through to the roof deck. And, of course, these same limbs need to be regularly trimmed to avoid damage during high-wind conditions. Power washing and zinc strips nailed along the centre ridge also can help reduce moss conditions.

Metal flashings with rust damage can cause leaks. Flashings seal the roof wherever the roofline is interrupted – around vents, chimneys, skylights and in valleys. Repair or replace the flashing as necessary.

Finding Roof Leaks

While the general condition of a roof can give you a sense of its potential for leaking, pinpointing the source of an actual problem calls for swift and immediate action. Of course, some problems are readily apparent on the roof itself. Other cases involve closer internal inspection. Examine rafters and sheathing. In addition to locating any drips or moisture, look for discolouration, streaking and rotting. Mark these areas at their highest point and their relative proximity to a chimney, vents or other roof elements so you can easily locate them.

Emergency Repairs

Use a plywood sheet for an emergency cover and double-headed nails to temporarily secure it.

Plastic sheeting or a tarp also can be used to cover roof damage. Hold plastic edges down with nailed strips of lath until the roof can be fixed. In all cases, patch holes with roof mastic after removing the nails.

Reducing Damage from Ice Dams

Ice dams occur when melting snow refreezes near the eaves, causing ice to back up under the shingles and melt onto the sheathing. The key to prevention is to keep the attic heat to a minimum with adequate ventilation and insulation.

If you already have a problem with ice backup, melt a channel through the ice with hot water. This allows the water to flow off the roof before it freezes. If this fails to alleviate the problem, bring in a professional to steam ice away. Using force and sharp objects like ice picks can do more damage than good on a cold, brittle roof.

Minimizing Water Damage

If water flows down toward a wall, nail a small block of wood in the water trickle on the attic rafters or sheathing to direct dripping water into a bucket.

To limit the extent of water damage, drive a Mastercraft awl or a nail into the centre of a ceiling water stain and put a bucket under it.

Shingle & Flashing Repairs

You will be happy to know roof materials that have sustained minimal damage or wear can be easily patched or repaired, thus avoiding replacement. Plastic roof cement and rolled, galvanized flashing can be used for many simple roof repairs.

How to Shingle Over an Old Roof

1 Cut tabs off shingles and install the remaining strips over the reveal area of the old first course, creating a flat surface for the starter row of new shingles. Use 1¼"-long roofing nails.

2 Trim the tops off shingles for the first course. The shingles should be sized to butt against the bottom edges of the old third course, overhanging the roof edge by ½". Install the shingles so the tab slots do not align with the slots in the old shingles.

3 Using the old shingles to direct your layout, begin installing the new shingles. Maintain a consistent tab slot offset. Shingle up toward the roof ridge, stopping before the final course. Install flashing as you proceed. If the valley flashing is in good condition, it does not need to be replaced.

4 Replace old flashing during the shingling sequence. A "roofover" is flashed using the same techniques and materials used for shingling over building paper, except you need to trim or fill in shingles around vent pipes and roof vents to create a flat surface for the base flange of the flashing pieces.

5 Tear off old hip and ridge caps before shingling the hips and ridge. Replace old hip and ridge caps after all other shingling is completed.

How to Replace a Shingle

1 Raise the edge of the damaged shingle. Use a slim pry bar to remove nails holding the shingle.

2 Insert a new shingle and align it with adjacent shingles. Peel away the liner that covers the adhesive on the back of the shingle.

3 Drive galvanized roofing nails near each side and at the top of each slot on the new shingle. Nail heads should be covered by overlapping shingles.

4 Dab roof mastic over each nail and press shingles flat. The sun's heat will activate the mastic and create a seal.

Use plastic roof cement for a variety of minor repairs, like reattaching loose shingles. Wipe down the building paper and the underside of the shingle, let them dry and then apply roof cement liberally. Seat the shingle in the bed of cement.

Working with Shingles & Roof Cement

Tack down buckled shingles *by cleaning out below the buckled area, filling the underside of the shingle with roof cement and pressing it down. Use roof cement to patch cracks or other minor shingle problems as well. It helps to use a hair drier to soften old shingles before working with them.*

New replacement shingles *can be made to look older by wiping them with mineral spirits. Seal gaps around roof flashing by cleaning out the old roof cement and replacing it with new. Joints around flashing are common places for roof leaks to occur.*

How to Replace a Section of Shingles

1 Pull out damaged shingles in the repair area, beginning with the uppermost shingle. Be careful not to damage any surrounding shingles that are in good condition.

2 Remove old nails with a flat pry bar. Exposed nail heads will cause punctures in new shingles. It is also important to remove nails in the shingle above the repair area to enable you to nail new shingles. Cover holes or damage in the building paper with roof cement.

3 Install replacement shingles, beginning with the lowest shingle in the repair area. Nail above tab slots with 7⁄8" or 1" roofing nails.

4 Install all but the top shingle with nails, then apply roof cement to the underside of the top shingle, above the seal line.

5 Slip last shingle into place under the overlapping shingle. Press the shingle into the roof cement. Lift up the shingle above the repair area and nail the top replacement shingle into place.

How to Replace Wood Shakes & Shingles

1 Split the damaged shake or shingle using a hammer and chisel. Remove the pieces and then pry out nails. For nails in overlapping shingles, cut them with a hacksaw blade slipped underneath the shingle.

2 Gently pry up shingles or shakes above the repair area. Cut new shingles or shakes for the lowest course, leaving about ⅜" for expansion. Nail replacement pieces in place with ring-shank siding nails (photo right). Fill in all but the top course.

3 Cut pieces for the top course and slip them beneath the overlapping shingles. Face-nail them in place near the tops. Cover all exposed nail heads with roof cement, then wipe off any excess. Use wood sealer or stain to give the new material a "weathered" look.

How to Replace Step Flashing

1 Carefully bend up counter flashing (or pry out siding) covering the damaged step flashing. Cut roof cement seals and pull back the shingles covering damaged step flashing. Remove the damaged piece or pieces of flashing with a flat pry bar.

2 Cut new step flashing from the same type of metal (aluminum or galvanized steel) used for the old flashing. Apply roof cement to the flashing on both exposed sides. Slip the flashing into place, making sure it is overlapped by the flashing above it and that it overlaps the flashing below. It also must overlap the shingle beneath it. Drive one roofing nail through the flashing at the bottom corner and into the roof deck. Do not fasten to the roof element.

3 Bend counter flashing back down and seal the seams with roof cement.

4 Lift shingles next to the repair area, then apply fresh roof cement to the undersides and to any exposed nail heads. Press the shingles down against the flashing to create a bond. Do not nail flashing when attaching shingles.

How to Patch Damaged Flashing

1 Measure the damaged area and cut a patch from similar material. The patch should be wide enough to slip under the shingles at each side of the repair area. Break the seal between flashing and shingles and wire-brush the damaged flashing.

2 Apply a bed of roof cement to the back side of the patch, then slip it under the shingles. Press the patch securely into the roof cement. Add cement at the seams and shingle joints, feathering it out to prevent damming of water.

> **TIP:**
> Loose flashing can be caused by external forces like high wind, or by failure of sealant or fasteners. Damaged and deteriorated flashing are primary causes of roof leaks.

Repairing Fascia & Soffits

Few things do more to ensure a healthy roof than an efficient, well-ventilated soffit and fascia system. It adds a finished look, prevents moisture from building up under the roof and in the attic, and stops pests from nesting in the eaves.

Fascia is attached to rafters or rafter lookouts (photo right). Beyond cosmetics, fascia provides a stable surface for eaves-troughs.

Repair by cutting out and replacing the damaged material. Joints between fascia boards are lock-nailed, so you should remove whole sections of fascia to make accurate mitre cuts for patches. Soffits usually are not removed for repairs.

Fasten material with ring-shank siding nails or galvanized deck screws.

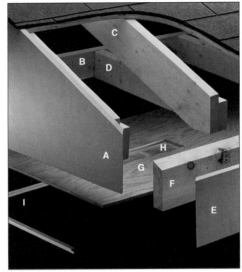

Some soffit types *attach to fascia headers while others fit into grooves cut in the back sides of the fascia. Elements include: a cornice cover (A); ledger board (B); rafter (C); rafter lookout (D); fascia (E); fascia header (F); soffit panel (G); soffit vent (H); and soffit moulding (I).*

RECOMMENDED POWER TOOLS

MASTERCRAFT
CIRCULAR SAW

MASTERCRAFT
JIGSAW

MASTERCRAFT
DRILL

RECOMMENDED HAND TOOLS

- basic hand tools
- flat pry bar
- chisel
- nail set
- screwdriver bits

NEEDED MATERIALS

- matching replacement materials
- nailing strips
- nails or screws
- caulk
- primer
- paint

How to Repair Tongue-and-Groove Soffits

1 Remove the soffit moulding. Cut out the damaged section as close as possible to the rafter lookout. Pry the damaged section loose. To remove tongue-and-groove that runs the width of the soffit, cut across the ends of the boards near the fascia (photo right).

2 Cut a nailing strip from 2x2 stock and use 2½" galvanized screws to attach to lookouts at opening ends.

3 Cut patch boards to fit using similar stock. Fasten all but the final board by driving 8d galvanized nails through pilot holes in the tongues of the boards and into the nailing strips. Set the nail heads so the next patch board will fit cleanly over the tongue of the first board.

4 Trim the top lip from the grooved edge of the last board in the sequence. Position the board in the opening and face-nail ring-shank siding nails through the last patch board and into the nailing strips. Prime and paint, and attach vent covers.

After locating look-outs *on each side of the damaged area, drill an entry hole and use a Mastercraft jigsaw to remove material.*

DECK REPAIRS

RECOMMENDED POWER TOOLS

MASTERCRAFT
CIRCULAR SAW

MASTERCRAFT
DRILL

RECOMMENDED HAND TOOLS

- basic hand tools
- flat pry bar
- awl
- chisel
- eye protection
- scrub and paintbrushes
- pressure sprayer
- hydraulic jack
- 5/8" masonry bit
- level
- ratchet wrench
- screwdriver bits

NEEDED MATERIALS

- sealer-preservative or staining sealer
- galvanized nails (6d, 10d)
- deck lumber
- baking soda
- corrosion-resistant deck screws
- 5/8" masonry anchor
- 3/8" lag screw
- concrete block
- scrap plywood

Like decks themselves, deck repairs serve both a cosmetic and a practical function. You will enhance the look of your deck by replacing old, weather-worn boards. At the same time, replacing rotted or damaged stairs, joists and deck boards can eliminate safety hazards and recapture the strength and integrity of the original structure.

Another good reason to replace or reinforce damaged deck wood as soon as possible is to halt the advance of wood rot, which can spread and weaken solid wood.

After replacing or reinforcing the rotted wood, clean the entire deck and apply a fresh coat of clear sealer-preservative or staining sealer. Apply a fresh coat of finish each year to prevent future water damage (photo below left).

TIP:
If existing decking is grey, you can create a similar "weathered" colour on the replacement wood by scrubbing it with a solution made from one cup baking soda and a gallon of warm water. Rinse and let dry.

How to Renew a Deck

1 Mix deck-brightening solution as directed by the manufacturer and apply it with a pressure sprayer. Let the solution set for 10 minutes.

2 Scrub the deck thoroughly with a stiff scrub brush. Wear rubber gloves and eye protection.

3 Rinse the deck with clear water. If necessary, apply a second coat of brightener to extremely dirty or stained areas. Rinse and let dry.

4 Apply a fresh coat of sealer or stain every year.

Clean debris from the cracks between decking boards with a putty knife. Debris traps moisture and can cause wood to rot.

Drive new fasteners to secure loose decking to joists. If using the old nail or screw holes, new fasteners should be slightly longer than the originals.

How to Repair Decking & Joists

1 Remove nails or screws from the damaged decking board, using a nail puller or screwgun. Remove the damaged board.

2 Inspect the underlying joists for signs of rotted wood. Joists with discoloured soft areas should be repaired and reinforced.

3 Use a hammer and chisel (photo below left) to remove any rotted portions of a joist.

4 Apply a thick coat of sealer-preservative to the damaged joist. Let it dry before applying a second coat. Cut a reinforcing or sister joist from pressure-treated lumber.

5 Treat all sides of the sister joist with clear sealer-preservative and then let dry. Position the sister joist tightly against the damaged joist and attach with 10d nails, driven every 2'.

6 Attach the sister joist to a ledger and header joist by toenailing with 10d nails (photo below right). Cut replacement decking boards from matching lumber using a circular saw or power mitre saw.

7 Apply a coat of sealer-preservative or staining sealer to all sides of the new decking board.

8 Position the new decking and attach it to joists with galvanized deck screws or nails. Make sure space between boards matches that of existing decking.

Remove wood rot *as soon as possible to keep it from spreading to solid wood sections.*

This sister joist *reinforces rotted or otherwise damaged deck joists.*

How to Replace Posts

1 Build a support using plywood scraps, a concrete block and a hydraulic bottle jack (photo below left). Place a 1½" layer of plywood between the head of the jack and the beam. Apply just enough pressure to slightly lift the beam.

2 Remove the nails or lag screws holding the damaged post to the anchor pad and to the beam. Remove the damaged post and the wood anchor pad on the concrete pier.

3 Drill a hole in the middle of the concrete pier using a hammer drill and a ⅝" masonry bit. Insert a ⅝" masonry anchor into the hole.

4 Position a galvanized post anchor on the pier block (photo below right) and thread a ⅜" lag screw and washer through the hole in the anchor and into the masonry anchor. Tighten the screw with a ratchet wrench.

5 Using a framing square, mark and then cut a new post from pressure-treated lumber. Treat cut ends with sealer-preservative. Position the post and make sure it is plumb.

6 Attach the bottom of the post to the post anchor using 6d galvanized nails. Attach the post to the beam by redriving the lag screws, using a ratchet wrench. Release the pressure on the jack and remove the support.

RECOMMENDED POWER TOOLS

MASTERCRAFT

CIRCULAR SAW

RECOMMENDED HAND TOOLS

- basic hand tools
- ratchet wrench
- framing square
- masonry drill bits
- hydraulic bottle jack
- level

NEEDED MATERIALS

- metal post anchor
- post lumber
- 6d galvanized nails
- concrete block
- plywood scraps

Use a hydraulic bottle jack to create temporary support when replacing posts. They are available in 2- to 20-ton sizes, with lift capacities ranging from 7⅛" to 13⅝" for the 2-ton jack, and from 9½" to 18⅝" for the 20-ton jack.

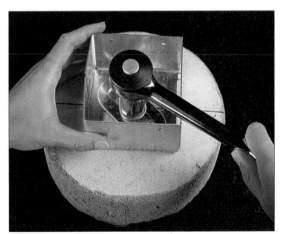

Galvanized post anchors like the one being installed above are used to hold the new posts in place.

The Mastercraft tools and accessories featured in this book have been provided by Canadian Tire. Visit a Canadian Tire Store near you for a wide assortment of Mastercraft tools and accessories to assist you in your home repair, maintenance and improvement projects.

Index

A

Aluminum siding, see Metal siding
Asbestos shingles, 12
Asphalt care & repair, 46, 47
Attic ventilation
    and ice dams, 53
    and shingle damage, 52

B

Basement moisture problems, 31, 48
    preventing, 49, 52
Boxing paints, 25
Brick moulding, replacing, 17
Brick veneer, repairing, 12, 13
Brushes, see: Paintbrushes

C

Caulk
    how to apply, 10
    masonry products, 11, 30, 31
Ceiling, minimizing water damage from leaky roof, 53
Chimney
    caulking for, 11, 30
    chimney cap repairs, 34
    damaged mortar cap, 30, 34
Cleaning painting tools, 25
Concrete
    cleaning & maintenance, 45
    disguising repairs, 38
    repairing, 37-46
    resurfacing, 42, 43
    sealing, 39, 45
    troubleshooting, 37, 39
Cracks
    in concrete, 39-41, 46
    in siding, 10-15, 21
Crazing of concrete, 39

D

Deck
    maintenance, 58, 59
    repairing, 58, 60, 61

    replacing post, 61
    safety, 58, 59
    weathering new wood to match old wood, 58
Door
    caulking around, 11, 21
    inspecting, 13
    painting, 27
    replacing brick moulding, 17
Downspouts, splash block for, 49
    see also: Eavestrough system

E

Eavestrough system
    and paint failure, 19
    as cause of wet basement, 31, 48
    gravel in, 52
    maintenance, 49
    painting, 26
    rehanging, 48
    repairing, 48-51
    snap-together vinyl, 51
Efflorescence on masonry, 19, 30
    removing, 35
Egg splatter, removing, 35
Electrical service safety, 9

F

Fascia, 52
    painting, 26
    repairing, 57
Fibreglass insulation as backing for caulking, 11
Flashings, 52
    caulking, 11
    repairing, 52, 55, 56
    replacing, 54, 56
    rust damage, 52
    sealing, 55
Foundation
    caulking around, 46
    caulking mud sill, 11
    directing water away from, 49, 52
    grading soil around, 29, 31
    painting, 26
Freeze-thaw cycle, 29, 30, 39, 53
Frost heave, 39

G

GFCI receptacles & extension cords, 9
Grading soil around foundation, 29, 31
Gutters, see: Eavestrough system

H

Holes in concrete, repairing, 41, 42
Hydraulic bottle jack, 61

I

Ice dams, 53
Iron stains on masonry, removing, 35
Ivy, removing from masonry, 35

J

Joists for deck, repairing, 60

L

Lacquer thinner, safety, 25
Ladder safety tips, 9
Latex paint, 19
    clean-up, 25
Lead-based paint, 19
Leak in roof, 19, 53
    causes, 56

M

Masonry
    efflorescence, 19, 30, 35
    cleaning & painting, 23, 26, 35, 36, 38
    painting, 35, 36, 38
    refacing damaged block, 33
    reinforcing bad block section, 33
    removing old paint, 22
    removing stains, 35
    repairing, 11, 12, 31-34
    replacing damaged brick, 32, 33
    tools for repairing, 29
    troubleshooting, 29, 30
    tuckpointing, 30-32
    veneer, repairing, 45
Masonry anchor, resetting, 44
Metal siding, 13
    painting, 23
    removing old paint, 22
    repairing, 12, 14, 16
Mildew on painted surface, 19
Mineral spirits
    safety, 25
    using to make new shingles match old, 55
Moisture, 56
    basement, 31, 48